GATHER UP THE FRAGMENTS

A ONE MONTH DEVOTIONAL

GATHER UP THE FRAGMENTS

A ONE MONTH DEVOTIONAL

by

Paul Cartwright

40 Beansburn, Kilmarnock, Scotland

ISBN-13: 978 1 914273 24 7

40 Beansburn, Kilmarnock, Scotland

www.ritchiechristianmedia.co.uk

Typeset by John Ritchie Ltd., Kilmarnock
Printed by Bell & Bain Ltd., Glasgow

CONTENTS

"Therefore, my beloved brethren, be ye stedfast, unmoveable, always abounding in the work of the Lord, forasmuch as ye know that your labour is not in vain in the Lord."

1 Corinthians 15.58

FOREWORD

"Teach me thy way, O Lord; I will walk in thy truth." (*Psalm 86 v 11*)

Of course, a devotional can be used by all, but specifically for a young or new believer it can help focus and structure their thoughts, without becoming a replacement for their Bible in their daily readings.

This book is a collection of short devotions or words in season which were used to encourage fellow believers during the coronavirus pandemic. Some of these were originally gospel related and were shared on social media platforms but have now been revised to provide a more devotional feel.

As these fragments of thoughts were gathered in weekly baskets, it was suggested that they should be brought together in a devotional format, so as to share them with a wider audience. Each day commences with a short passage of Scripture and the thirty-one daily devotions cover topics such as The Songs of Scripture, His Cross and Essentials for Outreach.

My heart's desire is that these gathered up fragments from the Holy Scriptures may provide believers in the Lord and Saviour Jesus Christ with some short, but fresh, daily manna.

May the Lord's name be glorified as we "***Consider Him***".

Paul Cartwright

DEVOTIONALS

DAY 1	*But he saith unto them, It is I; be not afraid.* John 6.20

Bible Reading: John 6.16-21

As we weather the storms of life, we can look to the Bible for encouragement and help. One example is in John chapter 6, verses 16 to 21, where we read of the Lord Jesus and His disciples during a storm on the Sea of Galilee.

As we read this passage, we firstly notice '**The Setting**'. The Lord had instructed the disciples to get into a boat and to sail over to the other side. It had been a busy day after the feeding of the 5,000 but now the disciples were in a *"**dark**" (v17)* place. Sometimes, as we look around and as we look out into the world, we can see this darkness in our lives. We see the sin and evil in man's heart in the world all around us and, like these disciples, we find ourselves in a dark place.

As we continue through the passage, we are taken up with '**The Sea**'. At the beginning, we see the calmness of the sea as they set sail, but *"**the sea arose**" (v18)*. In our lives we can look back and see the calmness of life but then events take hold, and, like the sea, our boat of life starts to rock.

We can note that the sea not only arose, but the disciples realised they were now in the middle of '**The Storm**', with *"**a great wind that blew**" (v18)*. Maybe today in our life we feel the cold winds of the north and as the sea is rocking our boat of life we can easily be taken up with the winds, distress, turmoil of our surroundings and maybe now you are experiencing a storm in your life.

What was the disciples' reaction? They "***toiled in rowing***" *(Mark 6 v 48)* and here we are presented with '**The Struggle**'.

They were hardened fishermen but even they struggled to bring the boat under control. As we experience life's challenges, we may be struggling. Maybe we are struggling to cope with the darkness and storm going on around us and like the disciples are trying to row and struggle our way out of the storm.

We have considered the setting, the sea, the storm and the struggle. As we look back, we read of the disciples: *"**They were afraid**" (v19)*. In your current circumstances you may find yourself in this situation today, afraid, apprehensive of what the future holds, but let's remind ourselves of those comforting words spoken in verse 20 by '**The Saviour**' to His disciples – *"**It is I, be not afraid**"*. They welcomed Him into their boat and the storm and wind ceased and they landed safely on the other side. May we encourage our hearts that if the Lord Jesus is in our boat of life we can be assured of encouragement and help during the storms of our life. We will experience the storm but with the Lord by our side we need *"**not be afraid**"*.

NOTES

DAY 2	*Let the word of Christ dwell in you richly in all wisdom ... singing with grace in your hearts to the Lord.* Colossians 3.16

Bible Reading: Colossians 3.16

As we wake each morning, sometimes a song in our heart can invigorate us for the challenges that the day will have before us. Within the Scriptures there are many songs, both long and short, but as we look to Christ maybe we can turn to some of these songs which would represent milestones throughout His life.

We would turn to ***"The Song of Songs"***, the Song of Solomon, and particularly in chapter five where we have a clear devotional look at each characteristic and detail of His person – from the head of fine gold, His eyes being like doves, lips like lilies, hands as fine gold, legs as pillars of marble with the beautiful song building up to the great crescendo of the chorus - ***"He is altogether lovely"*** *(Song of Solomon 5 v 16).*

As we again view His perfect life, we look towards those that scorned our blessed Saviour and, as the man who was despised and rejected, He became ***"the song of the drunkards"*** *(Psalm 69 v 12).* Although He went on to endure the shame of the cross and died for our sins on the cross, He triumphantly arose from the dead on the third day.

The song of the present and the future is found in the book of Revelation 15 verse 3, ***"the song of the Lamb"***. Praising the Lamb of God throughout eternity with one accord, the song of heaven will ring out: ***"Worthy is the Lamb that was slain to receive power, and***

riches, and wisdom, and strength and honour, and glory, and blessing" *(Revelation 5 v 12).*

As we are exhorted in the book of Hebrews, to *"**Consider Him**" (Hebrews 12 v 3),* let our daily songs be taken up with praising and worshipping our Saviour as we sing ***"psalms and hymns and spiritual songs, singing and making melody"*** in our ***"hearts to the Lord"*** *(Ephesians 5 v 19)* and we will be found ***"singing with grace in"*** our ***"hearts to the Lord"*** *(Colossians 3 v 16).*

NOTES

DAY 3	*Christ also suffered for us, leaving us an example, that ye should follow his steps.* 1 Peter 2.21

Bible Reading: 1 Peter 2.21-22 & 24

We wonder and marvel at Christ's walk, words and work as He dwelt among men here on earth so many years ago. The example He left for us to follow is brought before us in the following three simple thoughts today in the first epistle of Peter and chapter two.

We can firstly consider and remember *"**His Steps**" (v21)* as He went about doing good, bringing blessing to the multitudes and to individuals. Those steps never faltered throughout His earthly ministry and that pathway led Him ultimately to the cross of Calvary and beyond.

Throughout that perfect and spotless walk of Christ, He spoke with power through *"**His Mouth**" (v22).* As the full verse reminds us, He ***"did no sin, neither was guile found in his mouth"***. Think of the time He raised Lazarus from the dead. ***"He cried with a loud voice, Lazarus come forth"*** *(John 11 v 43)* and the man who had been dead four days was raised from the dead. He also spoke softly and tenderly when required to bring encouragement in times of need or sorrow. There was never a word or action He had to retract, and the sweetness of His words are lovingly expressed in Song of Solomon chapter five – ***"his lips like lilies, dropping sweet smelling myrrh"*** *(Song of Solomon 5 v 13).*

As we retrace the footprints of the Saviour and consider His words, we are finally drawn to His work, the work His Father had given Him.

Peter writes, *"**Who his own self bare our sins in his own body on the tree**" (v24).* What a sacrifice He made to save us from a lost eternity and *"**by whose stripes ye were healed**"*. His body was *"**given**" (Luke 22 v 19)* and *"**broken**" (1 Corinthians 11 v 24)* at the place called Calvary so that we can be saved through the shedding of His precious blood. We can reflect, like the hymn writer of old – *"Hallelujah, What a Saviour!"*

So, with Christ as our example let us strive to walk in His steps today and sound out the wonderful message of the Gospel to those that we meet, and that we may glorify God in our bodies and in our spirits, *"**which are God's**" (1 Corinthians 6 v 20).*

NOTES

AS HE WAS, AS HE IS

DAY 4	*When he shall appear, we shall be like him; for we shall see him as he is.* 1 John 3.2

Bible Reading: Mark 4.36 & 1 John 3.2

Today, we would like to consider our Saviour in two aspects as we look back and then look forward with the two little phrases in our readings.

We can look back today and consider our blessed Saviour *"**as he was**"*. If we are saved through the grace of God, we can look back today on that dreadful, dark, and violent scene of Calvary, and can view afresh today the sufferings of our Saviour, who gave His life and died for our sins. We can consider the hatred of men as the *"**man of sorrows**"* was *"**despised and rejected of men**"* but *"**he was wounded for our transgressions; he was bruised for our iniquities: the chastisement of our peace was upon him; and with his stripes we are healed**" (Isaiah 53 v 3 and 5)*. However, through the midst of that dark scene we hear the loving words of our Saviour. *"**Then said Jesus, Father, forgive them; for they know not what they do**" (Luke 23 v 34).*

Those two disciples who walked and talked on the Emmaus road were more than likely discussing and reflecting on the same scene that we have just considered, and the Lord would encourage their hearts by saying, *"**Ought not Christ to have suffered these things, and to enter into his glory?**" (Luke 24 v 26)*. We rejoice today that our Saviour died for our sins and was buried and on that third day was triumphantly raised from the dead. The suffering was over. He was then carried up and received back into heaven.

We can look back on Him *"**as he was**"*, but we can look up today and with the eye of faith see Him *"**as he is**"* – no longer crowned with a crown of thorn but one who is crowned with glory and honour. The truth today though, as God's redeemed people through the work of His Son, is that we have an eternal hope through that finished work of Christ. Faith one day, maybe today, will give way to sight and we shall truly see Him not *"**as he was**"*, but *"**as he is**"*. What a day that will be when we see our blessed Saviour face to face.

"Beloved, now are we the sons of God, and it doth not yet appear what we shall be: but we know that, when he shall appear, we shall be like him: for we shall see him as he is" *(1 John 3 v 2).*

NOTES

DAY 5	*Take, eat: this is my body, which is broken for you: this do in remembrance of me.* 1 Corinthians 11.24

Bible Reading: John 12.21, Hebrews 2.9, 1 John 3.2

Each Sunday morning, as Christians, we have the blessed opportunity and privilege to come together as the Lord's people with the sole purpose of remembering Him. Each week we remind our hearts of the words spoken by the Lord: *"**This do in remembrance of me**" (1 Corinthians 11 v 24)*, as we bring our praise, worship and thanksgivings to the Father for His blessed Son.

As we consider the phrase in John's Gospel today, do we come each Sunday morning with the gladness, joy and expectation that *"**We would see Jesus**"? (John 12 v 21).* Do we come prepared with our hands full and with our gathered baskets of fragments of the thoughts we have gleaned during the week in our private meditations? If we do, the expectation as we come to the Breaking of Bread will be our hearts' desire that *"**we would see Jesus**".*

If everyone in the assembly had this same desire, what a difference our Sunday services would be as we come to remember Him in His own appointed way. The Hebrew writer would go on to state: *"**We see Jesus**" (Hebrews 2 v 9).* What a wonder and experience we have when brethren audibly, and sisters inaudibly, bring their praise and worship during this time of remembrance.

During these blessed times, *"**we see Jesus**" (Hebrews 2 v 9)* as we consider and muse on the one that *"**was made a little lower than the angels for the suffering of death, crowned with glory and honour; that he by the grace of God should taste death for every man**" (Hebrews 2 v 9).*

As we partake of the emblems, the bread and the wine, we remember that we only do this until He comes. *"**For as often as ye eat this bread, and drink this cup, ye do shew the Lord's death till he come**" (1 Corinthians 11 v 26)* and what a blessed hope this is that one day faith shall give way to sight.

This would bring us to our final short phrase and as we have considered our preparation for the Breaking of Bread that *"**We would see Jesus**"*, during the time of remembrance *"**We see Jesus**"*, but finally one day we *"**shall be caught up together with them in the clouds, to meet the Lord in the air**" (1 Thessalonians 4 v 17)*. With this hope before us today we can be assured that one day *"**We shall see Him**" (1 John 3 v 2).*

Let us live today in the light of His soon coming and remind our hearts - **Perhaps Today!**

NOTES

DAY 6	*A bundle of myrrh is my well-beloved unto me.* Song of Solomon 1.13

Bible Reading: Song of Solomon 1.13

In the Bible there are many references to a wide range of fragrances, especially in the book of Song of Solomon where the book is full of scents, fragrances, and other oriental aromas.

At the outset and throughout the fragrant life of the Lord Jesus here on earth, the precious substance of myrrh was associated with Him. In the house, when He was a young child, the wise men came in and they ***"fell down, and worshipped him: and when they had opened their treasures, they presented unto him gifts; gold, and frankincense, and myrrh"*** *(Matthew 2 v 11).*

As the Shulamite maiden considered her beloved one in the Song of Solomon, these words are often associated with the Lord Jesus and describe His ways and perfect path in the world. ***"His cheeks are as a bed of spices, as sweet flowers: his lips like lilies, dropping sweet smelling myrrh"*** *(Song of Solomon 5 v 13).*

Throughout His life, He ***"went about doing good"*** *(Acts 10 v 38)* and many loving words were given to individuals and multitudes through His teaching. The fragrance of His person was expressed through the many ***"miracles and wonders and signs"*** *(Acts 2 v 22)* and the sweet fragrance of myrrh was evident through the loving words from His lips and the love for the people around Him.

As He hung on the cross, outside the great city of Jerusalem, there were those at the foot of the cross ***"and they gave him to drink wine mingled with myrrh: but he received it not"*** *(Mark 15 v 23).* During that dark and violent scene ***"at the place of a skull"*** *(Mark 15 v 22)* the fragrance of myrrh would have been lingering in the air as the Lord Jesus Christ ***"died for our sins"*** *(1 Corinthians 15 v 3).*

The Lord Jesus died, and His body was lovingly laid in a tomb by Joseph of Arimathaea and Nicodemus. They ***"brought a mixture of myrrh and aloes, about a hundred pound weight"*** *(John 19 v 39)* and they would have carefully and reverently taken the body and ***"wound it in linen clothes with the spices"*** *(John 19 v 40).*

On the third day, the Lord Jesus arose from the dead and was seen by many. Again, the fragrance of myrrh would have been evident from the spices and aloes applied during His burial a few days before.

As we consider the perfect life, death, and resurrection of the Lord Jesus we can be taken up with the fragrance and sweetness of Him and, with the words from the Bride, can state: ***"A bundle of myrrh is my well-beloved unto me".***

NOTES

DAY 7	*And when they were come to the place, which is called Calvary, there they crucified him.* Luke 23.33

Bible Reading: Luke 23.33-49

Philip Doddridge, in 1737, wrote the first line of his hymn, "*Behold, the amazing sight*", but what was he writing about and what was so amazing about this sight?

The first thing we need to consider is '**The Place**' where this great event happened. In Luke 23, we read about the location and the sight. It reminds us in verse 33, ***"And when they were come to the place, which is called Calvary, there they crucified Him"***. The 'Him' of this verse and the sight the hymn writer is referring to is the Lord Jesus Christ, who, having done nothing wrong, was taken and nailed to a cross to be crucified. Doddridge's hymn continues from the first line: "*The Saviour lifted high*".

Later in the chapter, in verse 48, we read, ***"And all the people that came together to that sight, beholding the things which were done, smote their breasts, and returned"***. We can be drawn to '**The Gathering**' - ***"all the people that came together"***. What a gathering this was with religious leaders, soldiers, and general men and women of the day. All had come to see this spectacle and to behold the sight that Jesus of Nazareth was to be put to death.

Varying people of different social, cultural and national backgrounds were represented at the foot of Calvary, and all were drawn to watch the ***"amazing sight"***, whether in derision, pity or because of simple curiosity.

Considering **'The Sight'**, the people had come together ***"to that sight"***, and what a sight it was. The original word for ***"sight"*** in this verse is found nowhere else in the Bible and we can only imagine what these people saw as they looked on ***"the things which were done"***. The Lord Jesus was ridiculed and rejected by men, buffeted, mistreated and the Bible states His back was like a ploughed field after all the whipping and scourging of the Roman soldiers: ***"The ploughers ploughed upon my back: they made long their furrows"*** *(Psalm 129 v 3)*. The soldiers had placed a crown of thorns upon His head, they had plucked the hairs from His cheeks. They then hammered nails into His hands and feet and lifted Him up on a cross. Anyone looking on the sight would see a scene of hatred, violence and cruelty, but in the very midst we hear words of love from the Lord Jesus Christ as He hung on the cross: ***"Father, forgive them; for they know not what they do"*** *(v34)*.

'The Reaction' of the people to this amazing sight was they ***"smote their breasts, and returned"***. At the place called Calvary, after they had beheld ***"the things which were done"***, they went away changed and there was a clear reaction to what they had seen and heard. Earlier in the chapter, the Centurion had observed ***"that sight"*** too and reacted as ***"he glorified God, saying, Certainly this was a righteous man"*** *(v47)*. I wonder what your reaction today is to ***"the amazing sight"*** of Calvary, the day that the Lord Jesus Christ died for you.

NOTES

DAY 8	*God shall wipe away all tears from their eyes.* Revelation 7.17

Bible Reading: John 11.1-36

During the life of our blessed Lord there were three occasions when our Saviour wept. It's encouraging to muse upon the fact that we have a Saviour who is touched *"**with the feeling of our infirmities**" (Hebrews 4 v 15).* As we consider the humanity of Christ in the Gospel of John, we see Him *"**Walking**"* in chapter 1, being *"**Weary**"* at the well in chapter 4, *"**Writing**"* in chapter 8 and *"**Weeping**"* at a graveside in chapter 11.

In chapter 11, we read the shortest verse in the King James Version Bible – *"**Jesus Wept**"*. This shows the love that He had for His people and His friends – the people looked upon Him as He wept and said, *"**Behold how he loved him**" (John 11 v 36).* He looked on the scene of death and what the effects sin had on the world but with His power He brought life and peace to the occasion when He cried out, *"**Lazarus, come forth**"*. Immediately, the one who had been dead four days, and already subject to corruption, was raised from the dead.

Luke 19 verse 41 states about the Lord Jesus: *"**When he was come near, he beheld the city, and wept over it**"*. The verse reminds us of the great stoop that our Saviour made – He came, from the mansions of glory; He saw, the great need, and He wept. As He looked upon the great city of Jerusalem maybe He pondered the days ahead, the journey to be made, the effects of sin.

Hebrews 5 goes on to state: *"**with strong crying and tears unto him**" (v7)*, which would remind us of the journey He made. The perfect servant, the one who was *"**touched with the feeling of our infirmities**"*, was found in the garden of Gethsemane offering ***"up prayers and supplications with strong crying"***.

The journey continued and led Him to outside the city, to the cross of Calvary, and we hear the strong crying of the Saviour: ***"My God, my God, why hast thou forsaken me?"***, but culminating with the triumphant cry, the cry of the conqueror: ***"It is finished"***. The work of salvation was complete.

Let's take heart today that tears are only for a season, and we can rejoice with the words of the book of Revelation that, one day, we believe very soon, ***"God shall wipe away all tears"*** *(Revelation 7 v 17).*

NOTES

DAY 9	*Simon a Cyrenian, who passed by, coming out of the country ... to bear his cross.* Mark 15.21

Bible Reading: Mark 15.16-25

Simon was a simple countryman and visitor to Jerusalem as one *"**who passed by**"* but what a day when he met Christ. The phrase we would like to consider is '**His Cross**'.

'His Cross' - in relation to Salvation – Simon carried the physical piece of the Lord's Cross, but when he arrived at the place called Calvary, the burden was lifted. As with us, we carried the burden of sin, but this was lifted and rolled away through the finished work of Christ at Calvary. We can rejoice today in the finished work of Christ at the Cross.

'His Cross' - in relation to Worship – Simon the Cyrenian was compelled to help with carrying Christ's Cross. The act brought him close to Christ. His Cross does this, and we remember, predominantly each Sunday as part of the Breaking of Bread, the work He accomplished on the Cross. We are taken up close with His Cross both corporately as an assembly and individually to collectively worship Him.

'His Cross' – in relation to our Walk – His Cross held Simon in Christ's steps. Walking independently would have been difficult. If we waiver or stray in our lives, we need to get back to His Cross, back to Calvary. It will keep us in the ways and steps of the Lord.

'His Cross'– in relation to our Service – Simon was privileged to be linked to Christ's work. Simon couldn't deal with the sin problem; he wasn't going to die as a sacrifice for sin, but he could be linked to sharing His Cross. We, like Simon, can share our experience of Christ, the value of Calvary.

What an experience Simon had that day, and we are sure he would have told others of Christ.

Finally, as we have been taken up with His Cross, life's journey may not be smooth. It certainly wasn't for Simon because of the crowds, the shouting and the soldiers, but we need to follow Christ, in His steps, which is what Simon the Cyrenian did.

NOTES

DAY 10	*For I am the Lord, I change not.* Malachi 3.6

Bible Reading: Malachi 3.6

Although our world is ever changing, we can take comfort today that the God of the Bible does not change. Malachi confirms this, ***"I am the Lord, I change not"*** *(Malachi 3 v 6)*. The God of Noah, Abraham and Solomon is the same today as He was in their day.

As the world and environment continue to change around us, we can have peace with the God that never changes by trusting in His Son, the Lord Jesus Christ. Paul wrote in the book of Romans, ***"We have peace with God through our Lord Jesus Christ"*** *(Romans 5 v 1)*. People and environments change but our Saviour ***"Jesus Christ (is) the same yesterday, and today, and for ever"*** *(Hebrews 13 v 8)*.

In the 1000th chapter of our Bible, in John chapter 3 verse 16, we can read that great verse: ***"For God so loved the world that he gave his only begotten Son, that whosever believeth in him should not perish but have everlasting life"***.

The true Good News message of the Bible is the same today as it was preached by the early Christians and let us take the opportunity today to tell others of this never-changing message of love and of the work accomplished by our Saviour Jesus Christ.

NOTES

DAY 11	*What wisdom is this which is given unto him, that even such mighty works are wrought by his hands?* Mark 6.2

Bible Reading: Mark 6.1-6

Throughout the life of the Lord Jesus Christ, when He was here on earth, His Hands brought so much blessing to individuals and multitudes of people. Mark confirms, *"**he began to teach in the synagogue: and many hearing him were astonished, saying ...What wisdom is this which is given unto him, that even such mighty works are wrought by His Hands?**" (Mark 6 v 2).*

He restored the sight to the blind like the man in the early chapters of Mark: *"**after that he put His Hands again upon his eyes, and made him look up: and he was restored, and saw every man clearly**" (Mark 8 v 25).* Those that were unable to walk were healed and He dramatically changed people's lives through His teaching.

The Bible reminds us, *"**how God anointed Jesus of Nazareth with the Holy Ghost and with power: who went about doing good, and healing all that were oppressed of the devil; for God was with him**" (Acts 10 v 38).*

The Lord Jesus lived a perfect life, but an appointed time came when He would be taken and crucified upon a cross. So many years before this event this was prophesied by the Old Testament writers as we see in David's writings, *"**They pierced My Hands**" (Psalm 22 v 16),* indicating that His Hands would be nailed to a cross.

As we know, the reason why He died was to give us the opportunity to get right with God as He paid the price of our sin in full by shedding His precious blood. ***"God commendeth his love toward us, in that, while we were yet sinners, Christ died for us"*** *(Romans 5 v 8)* and ***"without shedding of blood is no remission"*** *(Hebrews 9 v 22).*

On the third day, He arose from the dead and was seen by many, and when He met with His disciples, they were at first afraid and troubled until the risen Lord spoke to them: ***"Behold My Hands and my feet, that it is I myself: handle me, and see;"*** *(Luke 24 v 39).*

The Lord Jesus then returned to Heaven. He gathered His disciples, ***"and he led them out as far as to Bethany, and he lifted up His Hands, and blessed them. And it came to pass, while he blessed them, he was parted from them, and carried up into heaven"*** *(Luke 24 v 50 and 51).*

Let us not take the attitude of the Roman governor, Pontius Pilate, who tried to wash his hands of his responsibility towards the Lord Jesus as he stood before the crowd, but to reach out with loving hands to tell others of Christ.

"When Pilate saw that he could prevail nothing, but that rather a tumult was made, he took water, and washed his hands before the multitude, saying, I am innocent of the blood of this just person: see ye to it" *(Matthew 27 v 24).*

NOTES

LOOK AND LIVE

DAY 12	*And it shall come to pass, that every one that is bitten, when he looketh upon it, shall live.* Numbers 21.8

Bible Reading: Numbers 21.1-9

We appreciate the dedication of our health and emergency services which we hope we will rarely use, but I wonder whether you have ever noticed the logo, the snake and the rod, which is often associated with the medical profession. It is often displayed on sides of ambulances, and it is shown on the logo of the World Health Organisation.

There have been many debates over the origins of these symbols going back to the times of the ancient Greeks. However, in Numbers chapter 21, we can see a clear biblical foundation.

The nation of Israel was on the move through the wilderness, and they began to speak against God and their leader, a man of God called Moses. During this time God sent fiery serpents into their camp and many of the company, after being bitten by these snakes, died. The people then came to Moses and realised they had spoken and sinned against the God of heaven.

Moses prayed to God, on behalf of the people, and God provided a way of salvation. He asked Moses to create and set up a fiery serpent on a pole. He then communicated that anyone who was bitten by the snakes and then looked upon the raised brass serpent on the pole would live.

In the New Testament, the Lord Jesus referred to this event. While speaking with Nicodemus, He declared: *"**As Moses lifted up the serpent in the wilderness, even so must the Son of man be lifted up**" (John 3 v 14).*

This was a direct reference by Christ to His coming death. At the place called Calvary, He would be lifted up to be crucified. He would pay the price of our sin by shedding His precious blood. The Lord Jesus later said in chapter 12 of the same book, *"**And I, if I be lifted up from the earth, will draw all men unto me**" (John 12 v 32).*

We can look back today with thankful hearts to the day we looked on the crucified one and lived.

NOTES

THE PEARL

DAY 13	*If any man be in Christ, he is a new creature: old things are passed away; behold, all things are become new.* 2 Corinthians 5.17

Bible Reading: Matthew 13.1-58

Throughout the Bible there are many gems and precious metals mentioned, but on one occasion the Lord Jesus spoke to His disciples about the ***"one pearl of great price"*** *(Matthew 13 v 46).*

A pearl starts as something worthless, a small grain of sand or grit which is an irritant and eventually makes its way inside the Oyster. The Oyster reacts and protects itself by surrounding the foreign body by secreting mother-of-pearl over it and a beautiful pearl is formed.

The merchant man, in the parable that the Lord Jesus taught, was seeking ***"goodly pearls"*** *(v45)* and when he had found ***"one pearl of great price, went and sold all that he had, and bought it"*** *(v46).*

A parable is sometimes explained as an earthly story with a heavenly meaning, and we can possibly see a picture of the Lord Jesus and ourselves in this story.

It reminds us that we are worthless sinners, who have fallen short of God's standard and ***"without Christ, being aliens"*** and ***"strangers"*** and ***"having no hope, and without God in the world"*** *(Ephesians 2 v 12).* We are just like the small, insignificant grain of sand in a mighty ocean.

The merchant man could be a picture of the Lord Jesus Christ, rich, and one who came *"to seek and to save that which was lost."* He paid that *"great price"* by giving His life on the cross and shedding His precious blood. ***"Christ died for our sins according to the scriptures; and that he was buried, and that he rose again the third day"*** *(1 Corinthians 15 v 3-4).*

By repenting of your sin and placing your faith and trust in the Lord Jesus Christ, you can have your sins forgiven. Like the grain of sand, once worthless, lost and hostile, but now being arrayed with ***"the garments of salvation"*** *(Isaiah 61 v 10).*

The pearl is a thing of beauty, and this is now how the Lord Jesus Christ sees a forgiven and saved individual. One who is now dressed in beauty, not their own, and as Paul states in his letter to the Corinthians: ***"If any man be in Christ, he is a new creature: old things are passed away; behold, all things are become new"*** *(2 Corinthians 5 v 17).*

NOTES

DAY 14	*For consider him that endured such contradiction of sinners against himself.* Hebrews 12.3

Bible Reading: Hebrews 12.3

Around 1782, Samuel Stennett wrote a hymn beginning: ***"To Christ, the Lord, let every tongue, Its noblest tribute bring"***. One line in the hymn declares: *"**Behold, the beauties of His face**"*. The face Samuel Stennett wrote about was the face of our blessed Saviour, the Lord Jesus Christ, and in these few moments let's *"**consider him**" (Hebrews 12 v 3)* and the beauties of His face.

In Matthew 17, we read how the Lord Jesus went up a mountain to pray and, in verse 2, we read of His face *"**Shining**"*. Throughout the Lord's perfect and sinless life, His glory shone forth and He was a beacon of light when He walked among men. In another gospel, He declared, *"**I am the light of the world**" (John 9 v 5).*

Many *"**miracles and wonders and signs**" (Acts 2 v 22)* were conducted by the Lord Jesus Christ, but the purpose for which He came into the world was to *"**save sinners**" (1 Timothy 1 v 15).* In Romans chapter 3, we are reminded, *"**For all have sinned**" (Romans 3 v 23).*

To complete the work of salvation He needed to go to the great city. Luke says that He *"**Stedfastly set His face to go to Jerusalem**"*. There He was rejected of men and when Herod arrayed Him in a gorgeous purple robe and brought Him before the people of the day, they shouted with one accord, *"**Away with him, crucify him**" (John 19 v 15).*

The soldiers scourged and whipped Him, and others placed a reed in His hand and mocked Him and He was so maltreated that the Bible states, ***"His visage (face) was so marred more than any man"*** *(Isaiah 52 v 14).*

The gospel writer reminds us that they ***"smote him with the palms of their hands"*** and they ***"Spat"*** in His face. Eventually, He was taken outside the great city of Jerusalem and crucified upon a cross. As we look into the face of the one who hung on the cross, we consider the great stoop He made to save us and we can revel in the fact that ***"God commendeth his love toward us, in that, while we were yet sinners, Christ died for us".***

The Lord Jesus died and was buried, but on the third day ***"God raised him from the dead"*** *(Acts 13 v 30)* and His face was ***"Seen"*** by many. A few days later He was received back up into heaven.

The word ***"behold"*** simply means "to fix the attention", and as we have fixed our attention on the beauties of His face, we can rejoice in the wonder that one day we shall see Him. *"Face to face - what will it be, When with rapture I behold Him, Jesus Christ who died for me?"* - Carrie Ellis Breck's hymn.

NOTES

DAY 15	*What shall I do then with Jesus which is called Christ? They all say unto him, Let him be crucified.* Matthew 27.22

Bible Reading: Matthew 27.11-26

Life is like a journey on a grand sailing ship where we are all travellers to an eternal destination.

In the book of Ecclesiastes, it states: ***"A time to be born"*** *(Ecclesiastes 3 v 2)* and this is where we embark on our sailing experience on the ocean of life. Some voyages are short, and some are long, but all ships of life eventually lead to a destination – where are you destined?

All ships need a compass and charts to guide them through the perils and challenges of the sea and in our life's journey we can depend on the firmly founded Word of God, the Bible. ***"Thy word is true from the beginning: and every one of thy righteous judgments endureth for ever"*** *(Psalm 119 v 160)*

The Bible confirms that from the beginning of life's journey we have all fallen short of God's standard and, like the Psalmist of old, we can all acknowledge, ***"Behold, I was shapen in iniquity; and in sin did my mother conceive me"*** *(Psalm 51 v 5).*

Due to this sin, our destination on our life's journey is a lost eternity in a place the Bible calls Hell, but wait, the Bible declares Good News, and if we change master mid-journey our final eternal destination will change. Through the work accomplished on the cross of Calvary by

God's Son, the Lord Jesus Christ, we can have our sins forgiven and our life's ship can be under a new Master and Captain. ***"For it became him, for whom are all things, and by whom are all things, in bringing many sons unto glory, to make the captain of their salvation perfect through sufferings"*** *(Hebrews 2 v 10)*.

Job realised his life's journey was swiftly passing, ***"Now my days are swifter than a post: they flee away ... They are passed away as the swift ships"*** *(Job 9 v 25 and 26)***.** As we feel the exhilaration of the wind through the ship's sails and we navigate on through childhood, teen years and adulthood we wonder where the years have gone.

As you sail on to your eternal destination, are you looking to land in the harbour of heaven? Trusting Christ will assure you of your sins forgiven and landing on the shores of heaven at the end of life's journey. As we cross the ocean of life, every ship will experience storms throughout its voyage but if we trust Christ as our Saviour and let Him be at the helm of our life, the ***"hope we have as an anchor of the soul,*** *(will be)* ***both sure and stedfast"*** *(Hebrews 6 v 19)*.

NOTES

DAY 16	*The grass withereth, the flower fadeth: but the word of our God shall stand for ever.* Isaiah 40.8

Bible Reading: Isaiah 40.8

The Bible is a '**Preserved**' book, written long ago but so relevant for today's world and its challenges. Many have tried to destroy the book over the centuries. King Jehoiakim in the Bible tried to destroy the Word of God with a penknife and fire, as he didn't like what he heard, but without success. The Bible remains the top-selling book in the world and has been translated into many languages so all can read the wonders and truth found within its pages.

The Bible is also a '**Perfect**' book as it was written by God – ***"The law of the LORD is perfect, converting the soul: the testimony of the LORD is sure"*** *(Psalm 19 v 7)*. The Holy Scriptures are not man made but God breathed. ***"For the prophecy came not in old time by the will of man: but holy men of God spake as they were moved by the Holy Ghost"*** *(2 Peter 1 v 21)*.

The Bible contains the full details of how our world came into being from the very first verse, ***"In the beginning God created the heaven and the earth"*** *(Genesis 1 v 1)* and provides a clear view of history. Throughout its pages it points to the Lord Jesus Christ. The New Testament introduces us to the Lord Jesus' life here on earth and the many miracles, signs and wonders that He did. John reminds us: ***"these are written, that ye might believe that Jesus is the Christ, the Son of God; and that believing ye might have life through his name"*** *(John 20 v 31)*.

The Bible is also a '**Powerful**' book as the Hebrew writer reminds us: ***"For the word of God is quick, and powerful, and sharper than any twoedged sword, piercing even to the dividing asunder of soul and spirit, and of the joints and marrow, and is a discerner of the thoughts and intents of the heart"*** *(Hebrews 4 v 12)* and can dramatically change people's lives.

Let us today take hold of this precious book and get to know it better.

NOTES

DAY 17	*I will come again, and receive you unto myself; that where I am, there ye may be also.* John 14.3

Bible Reading: John 11.20

In verse 5 of John 11, we read of the love of the Lord Jesus for the family at Bethany. Later in the chapter, the Lord Jesus performs a mighty miracle by raising Lazarus from the dead, even after his body had been in the tomb for four days. We can reflect that the Lord was also triumphantly raised from the dead and as the Gospel writers remind us, He was then later *"**Carried up**" (Luke 24 v 51)*, *"**Taken up**" (Acts 1 v 9)* and *"**Received up**" (Mark 16 v 19)* into heaven.

The Lord reminds us as He spoke to His disciples in John chapter 14, *"**I will come again**" (John 14 v 3)* but do we really live in the light of this blessed truth? The Lord is coming, and it could be today!

In John chapter 11, Martha had heard that the Lord Jesus was coming. The idea in the passage is that He was already on His way to Bethany, and Martha's reaction to this news invoked action on her part – she *"**went and met him**"*. When we consider that Jesus is coming, what is our reaction? Do we have a similar reaction to the news that He is coming? Are we active in the Lord's work, in whatever avenue of service He has called us?

The reaction of Mary, in this specific verse, seems to be so different – *"**but Mary sat still in the house**"*. Is this our reaction to the great truth that our Lord and Saviour is coming again? Do we tend to sit back, leave the work to others?

Let us ponder these simple thoughts in the light of His soon coming and let us be fully active in the Master's service.

"The LORD hath done great things for us; whereof we are glad … they that sow in tears shall reap in joy. He that goeth forth and weepeth, bearing precious seed, shall doubtless come again with rejoicing, bringing his sheaves with him" *(Psalm 126 v 3, 5 and 6).*

NOTES

DAY 18	*And the house was filled with the odour of the ointment.* John 12.3

Bible Reading: John 12.3

The Lord visited many homes during His time here on earth, including the homes of Zacchaeus and the man with the palsy, but the home of Lazarus and his two sisters in Bethany would most likely be the most visited one.

In John 12 verse 2, we get a view of a Christian home and marvel that ***"Lazarus was one of them that sat at the table with Him"***, the one who had been dead but had been raised to life by the Lord Jesus.

What a privilege as we gather on a Sunday morning, at the Breaking of Bread, with the table before us with the blessed emblems of the crucified present, pointing us back to Calvary. We were once like Lazarus, dead, spiritually dead in our sins, but we met Him, our lives were changed, and we are now alive in Christ.

The Song of Solomon reminds us: ***"Thy name is as ointment poured forth"*** *(Song of Solomon 1 v 3)*, and as we consider Mary's act of worship, what an act it was. She had brought a ***"pound of ointment"*** into the home *(v3)*, a year's wages. It was costly to her, it was her heart-felt desire, and her actions showed she had an appreciation of Christ as she worshipped Him.

As the casket of spikenard was broken open and she began to anoint our Saviour's feet, and then go on to wipe His feet with her hair, *"**the house was filled with the odour of the ointment**" (v3)*.

As we consider the various aspects and characteristics of Christ, the outpouring of our worship and praise should fill our house. The fragrance of Christ should go with us into our daily lives and others should be able to smell the spiritual sweet fragrance of worship and praise we have for our Saviour. As we live for Him, others should know our position with Christ and our homes will be a constant silent witness to others.

D. L. Moody once stated: *"If Christ is in the house, your neighbours will sure get to know it"*. May the people we interact with daily see Christ in our lives and in our homes.

NOTES

DAY 19	*The Lord God is my strength ... and he will make me to walk upon mine high places.* Habakkuk 3.19

Bible Reading: Habakkuk 3.19

Our Bible verse encourages us to walk upon high places with God just like Habakkuk did. He had placed his faith in God, knowing He would be his strength during difficult times.

As we consider the High Places, we can maybe picture that hike up the mountain, the struggle and energy as we climb but a sense of achievement as we reach the summit. As we stand, we can take in the pure and fresh mountain air around us giving us time to consider God.

As we look out over the scenery surrounding us, we can be taken up with the views of Him as we consider His creation. The book of Job reminds us to: ***"Stand still, and consider the wondrous works of God"*** *(Job 37 v 14).*

Standing on the summit, we can look down on the world below and sense the distractions of everyday life becoming smaller and more insignificant as we spend time alone in the presence of God.

Our verse also mentions our life's pathway in the picture of the Hind's feet. The Hind, a female deer, is a sure-footed mountain animal and wherever its front legs are placed its back legs follow suit as every step is taken carefully. It's comfortable walking in a meadow, through a valley, or on the side of a mountain. In whatever terrain, it has surety and stability.

With God as our guide, we can also be safe and eternally secure throughout our life's pathway by putting our faith and trust in Him. Whatever the terrain of life we walk through, we can be assured of His strength to carry us along and ***"He hath said, I will never leave thee, nor forsake thee"*** *(Hebrews 13 v 5)*. Habakkuk trusted in God and relied on Him to guide him through the many circumstances of life. Will you?

NOTES

DAY 20	*For thou wilt light my candle: the Lord my God will enlighten my darkness.* Psalm 18.28

Bible Reading: Psalm 18.28

As we turn our minds to the book of Psalms today and read Psalm 18 verse 28, what a precious thought that the God of heaven can enlighten our darkness.

Right from the first chapter of the Bible, through to the last chapter of the Bible, the metaphor of light and darkness is used to illustrate stark contrasts and to provide clear spiritual lessons to us. Sometimes, light is associated with good, compared to darkness as evil. Whilst at other times, light represents life, and darkness reminds us of death.

As we look around us today, God is rarely mentioned, and as we currently find ourselves in dark days there seems to be no light at the end of the tunnel, just more shades of darkness, confusion and uncertainty. While sometimes we may be unnerved by the darkness in the world, we can be assured that God's perfect light casts out fear.

Our verse reminds us that God provides the light source to illuminate this darkness, and this is His Word, the Bible. Another Psalm states: ***"Thy word is a lamp unto my feet, and a light unto my path"*** *(Psalm 119 v 105).*

Although the surroundings we find ourselves in currently may be dark, the Word of God provides us light to ***"enlighten our darkness"***. It can lighten the path and provide light, like a lamp before us, as we step forward into the future.

The Lord Jesus said: " ***I am the light of the world: he that followeth me shall not walk in darkness, but shall have the light of life"*** *(John 8 v 12).*

NOTES

DAY 21	*Looking unto Jesus the author and finisher of our faith.* Hebrews 12.2

Bible Reading: Psalm 34.5

Sometimes the cares and worries of the world get us down, but we can turn aside today and look to Christ to encourage our hearts.

"They looked unto him, and were lightened" *(Psalm 34 v 5).* The idea is as they looked unto Him, their spirits were lifted, and their faces were radiant. We can look to the Lord Jesus throughout His life. In the first chapter of the Gospel of John, for example, we read: ***"Looking upon Jesus as he walked"*** *(John 1 v 36)* and what a perfect walk before God and man. He was ever God's daily delight.

The perfect walk ultimately led to the cross and the Hebrew writer would remind us: ***"Looking unto Jesus the author and finisher of our faith ... endured the cross, despising the shame"*** *(Hebrews 12 v 2).*

We give thanks to God that ***"Christ died for our sins according to the scriptures; And that he was buried, and that he rose again the third day"*** *(1 Corinthians 15 v 3 and 4).*

As we ponder this great redemptive work, and the precious blood that was shed to save our souls, we can rejoice that He was raised triumphantly from the dead and one day we will see Him face to face. As we continue along the Christian pathway, let us be a people that are found looking in expectancy for our Lord's return. Let us be found,

"Looking for that blessed hope, and glorious appearing of the great God and our Saviour Jesus Christ" *(Titus 2 v 13).*

In the meantime, let's be about the Master's service and as our faces are radiant and aglow after looking upon Him, let us not be ashamed to tell others of Him and His work.

NOTES

DAY 22	*Therefore, my beloved brethren, be ye stedfast, unmoveable, always abounding in the work of the Lord.* 1 Corinthians 15.58

Bible Reading: 2 Kings 5.1-14

There are many servants brought before us in this passage and all would be a faint picture of the Christian as a servant of God.

Firstly, we have the '**King's servant**', Naaman, a great man, honourable to his master. He could be regarded as a picture of great men and women who have been honourable and consistent to their Master, the Lord Jesus Christ. Naaman was well known in the land, and we can all recount the lives of great men and women of faith today and throughout the ages.

Secondly, we are introduced to a ***"little maid"*** *(v2)*, a damsel with no status, no name or identity, other than she ***"waited on Naaman's wife"***. Some servants of God are unknown, but known only unto God. Their work is done in obscurity, away from the general eyes of man. This little maid was not named but is mentioned on the pages of Scripture and through her simple, and maybe to others insignificant, work, she was instrumental in bringing about the change in Naaman's life. We can all do something for God, however small, to tell others of Christ, and through this small work we may see changes in the lives of the unsaved.

Finally, we come to the '**Servants of Naaman**'. The message had been given to Naaman by Elisha's servant, ***"but Naaman was wroth"*** *(v11)*.

In verse 13 we read: *"**His servants came near, and spake unto him**"*. Is this not a little picture of a servant of God who in one-to-one situations can share Christ and explain the ways of God?

So, as we are servants of God, whether well known throughout the land, doing a little work or simply in one-to-one conversations, let us be ***"stedfast, unmoveable, always abounding in the work of the Lord, forasmuch as ye know that your labour is not in vain in the Lord"*** *(1 Corinthians 15 v 58).*

NOTES

DAY 23	*Put on the whole armour of God, that ye may be able to stand against the wiles of the devil.* Ephesians 6.11

Bible Reading: Daniel 10.1-12

Daniel experienced many adventures throughout his life, from interpreting dreams of great kings, prophesying great vivid events of the future, and even surviving a night in the den of lions. Daniel is affectionally known in Scripture as *"**a man greatly beloved**" (v11)* and he was known for his faith and prayer.

Today, we want to simply consider three postures through which each man or woman of God can learn vital lessons from this great man of faith –

'Worship' - The first posture is found in verse 9 and verse 15, *"**my face toward the ground**"*, and what a beautiful picture this is in relation to our Worship to our God. Have we worshipped Him today, or praised Him with thanksgiving for saving our souls?

'Prayer' - The second posture Daniel moved to was a position of prayer - *"**upon my knees**" (v10)*. Notice, the subtle change he made from being face down, reflective of being in worship, to gradually moving to being set upon his knees, the position of prayer. Throughout the book of Daniel, he was best known for being a faithful man of God but also a man of fervent prayer. It was D. L. Moody who stated, *"He who kneels the most stands the best"*.

'Stand/Service' - This would move us to the third posture when, in verse

11, Daniel moves from a position of worship, into a position of prayer and now stands - *"**stand upright**"*. In our world today, like in Daniel's, Christians need to stand upright in the ways of the Lord. As we move into service to tell others of the wondrous message of the Gospel, we would also need to put on the whole armour of God to *"**stand against the wiles of the devil**" (Ephesians 6 v 11)*. Paul continues his exhortation for us to, *"**Stand therefore, having your loins girt about with truth**" (Ephesians 6 v 14)*.

Simple lessons today, but let's be taken up with Worship, Prayer and Service towards our blessed God in these dark and difficult days.

NOTES

DAY 24	*For the Lord himself shall descend from heaven with a shout, with the voice of the archangel, and with the trump of God.* 1 Thessalonians 4.16

Bible Reading: Luke 2.41-52

This is an interesting passage of Scripture, where we consider the boy Jesus at the tender age of twelve years old. We can picture the entourage as the family and friends travelled to Jerusalem to be part of the *"**Feast of the Passover**" (v41)* and then as Joseph and His mother returned supposing that Jesus was still with them.

The first consideration is with this backdrop, not knowing He had stayed behind in Jerusalem, *"**they sought him**" (v44).* Is this not our first step of salvation? We realised we were sinners in the sight of a Holy God, and we *"**sought him**" (v44).*

Secondly, after some three days, *"**they found him**" (v46).* Some have sought Him for many a day but what a joy it is when after seeking the Lord, we find Him. We realised that at the cross of Calvary He died for our sins, and putting our faith and trust in Him we are saved.

As we consider the Lord Jesus, surrounded by the wise men of the day, we note that they *"**heard him**" (v47).* We are not taken up with the voices of the wise men and woman of the day, but we can hear His voice as we daily read the Scriptures. Throughout our Christian pathway we can delve into the Scriptures and, as these men were, we can be *"**astonished**"* with the great truths of the Bible.

Finally, in verse 48, *"**they saw him**"*. It was a great day when, with the eye of faith, we saw and trusted in Christ. However, what a day that will be when we shall see Him face to face, *"**We shall see him**" (1 John 3 v 2)* and can echo the thought in this verse: *"**they saw him, they were amazed**"*.

So, as we look back and onward in our Christian experience, we can be joyful that we *Sought Him,* and we *Found Him*. During our life's experience, we shall *Hear Him* and our eternal joy will be to *See Him* in a soon-coming day – **Perhaps Today!**

NOTES

DAY 25	*He is not here: for he is risen, as he said. Come, see the place where the Lord lay.* Matthew 28.6

Bible Reading: Mark 14.32-35, 15.22-25, 16.2-6

There are many places that the Lord Jesus passed through, but possibly the most poignant places would have been Gethsemane, Golgotha and the Garden tomb.

"To a place which was named Gethsemane" *(Mark 14 v 32)* - The word "Gethsemane" comes from the Hebrew, "gath", which is the word for press, and "shemen" which is the word for olive oil. The olive press would have been where olives from the Olive trees in the garden of Gethsemane would have been crushed and the oil would have flowed out and been collected. As our Lord found Himself in this garden, the place of the olive press, it would be an appropriate place. The Lord suffered ***"being in an agony"*** *(Luke 22 v 44)*. In His experience in the garden, He would have figuratively felt the heavy weight of the olive press, as He contemplated the burden of going to the cross of Calvary. His soul was ***"exceeding sorrowful unto death"*** (*Mark 14 v 34*).

As His suffering continued, we can imagine the olive press tighten for, ***"His sweat was as it were great drops of blood falling down to the ground"*** *(Luke 22 v 44)*. We read that after His time of prayer, ***"He rose up from prayer"***. John tells us that they ***"led him away"***.

"The place Golgotha" *(Mark 15 v 22)* – Three of the four Gospel writers draw us to Golgotha and each of them refers to it as a place of a skull.

Was this due to its shape or simply because it was a regular place of execution? It would have been a place of violence and hatred for our Lord as He endured the cross for us. The soldiers once done with their work of nailing our blessed Saviour to the cross sat down and ***"they watched him there"*** *(Matthew 27 v 36).* As we ponder on this scene, we hear the words of love from the Saviour's lips, ***"Father, forgive them; for they know not what they do"*** *(Luke 23 v 34).* It was Charles Spurgeon who stated as he contemplated the scene: *"A work done in a day, but wondered at forever".*

"The place where they laid him" *(Mark 16 v 6)* - John reminds us it was a garden (John 19 v 41) where the tomb was. As we retrace the footprints of the Saviour from Gethsemane, Golgotha and into the Garden – the Lord had suffered for over 15 hours.

Graves usually state: "Here lies ..." but not so with our Saviour, as the Scriptures clearly state, ***"He is not here"***. We, like the angel, can say today ***"He is risen, he is not here: behold the place where they laid him"***– the grave clothes were there but He had risen!

As we reflect on these three significant places, may they warm our hearts and help us to ***"Consider Him"*** *(Hebrews 12 v 3)* today.

NOTES

DAY 26	*I am the good shepherd: the good shepherd giveth his life for the sheep.* John 10.11

Bible Reading: John 10.1-5

The Lord Jesus Christ is called the *"**Great Shepherd**"* in the book of Hebrews, *(Hebrews 13 v 20)*, the *"**Chief Shepherd**"* in the first epistle of Peter *(1 Peter 5 v 4)* and the ***"Good Shepherd"*** here in the Gospel of John *(John 10 v 11)*. Today, we would like to consider six simple thoughts, on both the Shepherd and His sheep –

'The Sheep are Saved by Him' - Let us not lose the joy of this simple statement, that the Good Shepherd gave His life for the sheep. The Shepherd that was smitten, shed His precious blood to redeem us and through putting our faith in Him we are saved for both time and eternity.

'The Sheep are Shepherded by Him' - We were once lost and wandering sheep but now, through grace, we find ourselves safely in the fold. Enclosed and sheltered by our beloved Shepherd and cared for by Him each step of our lives.

'The Sheep hear His voice' - As we are close to our Good Shepherd, we can hear His voice. Through the daily reading of Scripture, it's wonderful to hear our Shepherd's voice. During Bible times, these sheepfolds would hold many sheep from different shepherds. When the time came for the shepherds to move on, they called their sheep and only their sheep heard and obeyed their voice.

'The Sheep have names' - Sometimes in this vast world of ours we can be lonely, simply feeling like another statistic in the vast population. However, this is not the case with our Shepherd. We are individually known by Him.

The one who created the vast universe is interested in His sheep and He *"**calleth his own sheep by name**" (v3).*

'The Sheep are led by Him' - In Bible times, the shepherd would lead his sheep out across vast areas and into green pastures. The same is the case with our Shepherd. *"**He leadeth them out**" (v3).* We are encouraged to follow His ways by obeying His voice, following His ways laid out in the Scriptures.

'The Sheep are guided by Him' - We have a Shepherd who leads and guides us and, as verse four reminds us, *"**He goeth before them**"*. Our Good Shepherd will lead us through the ups and downs of life, through death, if the Lord be not come, and into Heaven.

As we consider these few simple thoughts today, we can truly say with assurance, and with joy in our hearts that *"**The Lord is my Shepherd**" (Psalm 23 v 1).*

NOTES

DAY 27	*Behold, God is my salvation; I will trust, and not be afraid:* Isaiah 12.2

Bible Reading: Isaiah 12.2-3

Our text begins with the word: ***"Behold"***, and the writer is fixing our attention on what is to follow. Today as Christians we can be thankful for *four thoughts* in these two verses –

"Behold, God is my Salvation" - as we again ponder on the great work of salvation, we are a thankful people as we are sinners saved by grace. Salvation is personal and the writer reminds us: ***"God is my salvation; I will trust and not be afraid"***. We can trust Him with all the challenges of life. We are exhorted to ***"not be afraid"***.

God is not only our '**Salvation**', but also our '**Strength**'. This is both spiritual and physical strength to handle our day to day lives. Even though difficult times in our life will come, we can call upon ***"Jehovah (who) is my strength"*** *(v2).*

As we can each say that God is my '**Salvation**' and my '**Strength**', He should also be our '**Song**'. Each day bringing praise and worship to Him. Isaiah 5 verse 1 exhorts us: ***"Now will I sing to my wellbeloved a song of my beloved"***. Each day we are encouraged to be: ***"Speaking to yourselves in psalms and hymns and spiritual songs, singing and making melody in your heart to the Lord"*** *(Ephesians 5 v 19).*

Finally, the fourth point we need to consider in these verses is '**Service**' for Him. We can experience a time of refreshment as we enjoy the *"**wells of salvation**"* in the service of our God – notice not a *well*, singular, but *wells*, an abundance. A time to share the living water that will bring life to sinners in the finished redemptive work of Christ. Our service for Him should be with energy, enthusiasm and with joy: *"**with joy shall ye draw**" (v3).*

The Psalmist knew this joy: *"**They that sow in tears shall reap in joy**" (Psalm 126 v 5)* and as we sow the Word of God, and share the wonderful message of the Gospel, *"**I say unto you, that likewise joy shall be in heaven over one sinner that repenteth**" (Luke 15 v 7).*

Let us today, with joy, draw the water out of the wells of salvation.

NOTES

DAY 28	*And the Word was made flesh, and dwelt among us.* John 1.14

Bible Reading: John 21.25

There are 3,116,480 letters in our KJV Bible, making up 783,137 words. These words make up 39 books in the Old Testament and 27 books in the New Testament. Both accumulating to provide us with one complete, inspired book, we call The Bible.

As we look closer into our Bible, we see our Lord and Saviour is described as being a '**Letter**' – we see in the book of the Revelation He is referred to as the first and last letter in the Greek alphabet: ***"I am Alpha and Omega, the beginning and the end, the first and the last"*** *(Revelation 22 v 13).* One who has no beginning or end but in the fulness of time He came into our world to complete the great work of salvation.

As we discover in John: ***"In the beginning was the Word, and the Word was with God, and the Word was God"*** *(John 1 v 1).* Now He is not only known as a '**Letter**', the beginning and the end, but as the '**Word**'. We rejoice together today that ***"the Word was made flesh"*** *(John 1 v 14).* Through Him coming into this dark world and accomplishing the great redemptive transaction at the cross of Calvary we can place our faith in Him and be saved.

As we wonder at the many signs and miracles He did, and ponder on the many lives He changed during this life, here on earth, we know the Bible only accounts for a few of these occasions for John reminds us of the '**Library**' of books, when he writes in his last chapter in his gospel, *"**And there are also many other things which Jesus did, the which, if they should be written every one, I suppose that even the world itself could not contain the books that should be written. Amen**" (John 21 v 25).*

So, today as we consider our Saviour as the Letter, Word and Library let us strive for Christ to be the A to Z of our lives with the all-important book, the Bible, as our guide.

NOTES

DAY 29	*Where there is no vision, the people perish.* Proverbs 29.18

Bible Reading: Proverbs 24.30-32

Today is a time of reflection, a spiritual reflection on how we are going on for God. It is good to regularly review our garden, our spiritual garden, in the light of the verse we have read today.

Over recent days you may have let your spiritual garden fall into disrepair. Your daily Bible time has now been overgrown and entangled by the cares and concerns of the day. The once clear path of reading a daily passage of Scripture has been ***"all grown over"*** with the world's ***"thorns and nettles"***.

Our interactions with others may have caused our Christian enthusiasm to dampen. Our spiritual ***"stone wall"*** of testimony and growth may have taken a battering during the weather of recent days.

However, verse 32 of Proverbs 24 states: ***"Then I saw, and considered it well"***. Let us now take this opportunity to have a spiritual reawakening and reflect on where we are spiritually. Let's ***"receive instruction"*** from our passage of the Bible and review our spiritual garden.

Let's, with help from the Lord, cultivate and cut back the overgrown non-spiritual elements of our life, clear the unprofitable clutter we have amassed and repair and build up our ***"broken down"*** stone wall with thoughts of Him and His Word.

Let's continue, with new vigour, to sow the good Word of God, share Christ with others and as we water the Word with our prayers let's look to the Lord for fruit.

NOTES

DAY 30	*The harvest is past, the summer is ended, and we are not saved.* Jeremiah 8.20

Bible Reading: Jeremiah 8.20

As we look back over the years, we have seen the months rapidly roll by and we ponder on past and present days, but what of the future?

We prepare for many things in life, but have you prepared to meet God? A little book in the Old Testament of the Bible exhorts us to ***"Prepare to meet thy God"*** *(Amos 4 v 12).*

One day in the future we will meet God as either our Saviour or as our Judge: ***"As it is appointed unto men once to die, but after this the judgment"*** *(Hebrews 9 v 27).* These may be solemn things to consider but your eternal destination depends on what you do with God's Son, the Lord Jesus Christ.

The Lord Jesus came into the world, ***"For the Son of man is come to seek and to save that which was lost"*** *(Luke 19 v 10).* He lived a perfect life here on earth and performed many ***"miracles and wonders and signs, which God did by him"*** *(Acts 2 v 22),* healing the sick, giving sight to the blind and even raising people from the dead.

When God's appointed time came, He was crucified and died upon a cross outside the great city of Jerusalem. Through the shedding of His precious blood the price of our sin was paid in full for we are ***"not redeemed with corruptible things, as silver and gold ... but with the precious blood of Christ"*** *(1 Peter 1 v 18 and 19).*

The Lord Jesus was raised from the dead on the third day and, *"**If thou shalt confess with thy mouth the Lord Jesus, and shalt believe in thine heart that God hath raised him from the dead, thou shalt be saved**" (Romans 10 v 9).*

We do not know what the future holds but we know that God holds the future. So, what of the future? Will you get right with God? Will you have your sins forgiven today, and have a guaranteed eternal future in heaven by trusting in the Lord Jesus Christ?

NOTES

DAY 31	*And he said unto them, Go ye into all the world, and preach the gospel to every creature.* Mark 16.15

Bible Reading: Nehemiah 4.1-12

We live in a dark and difficult world, but we need to have the clear exercise as Christians to go out to tell others of the wonderful, good news message, that Christ died for our sins. The wise man wrote: ***"Where there is no vision, the people perish"*** *(Proverbs 29 v 18).* Let us with the help of God have a vision and burden for the unsaved in our own district, locality, and surrounding areas.

Today, we want to consider in this passage *three* simple essentials for outreach work and the first is for '**People**': ***"For the people had a mind to work"*** *(v6).* In other words, people with the desire to do God's work. We may not all be public platform preachers, but we should all have a desire to tell others of Christ. All can give a word in season to an unsaved family member, invite a friend or neighbours to an outreach meeting, or simply share a tract or calendar.

The second essential is that as individuals, and corporately as an assembly, we should be taken up with '**Prayer**': ***"We made our prayer unto our God"*** (v9). The power of prayer is often not appreciated but it is an essential element to outreach work. As prayer partners we can pray for openings and for understanding the ways in which the Lord would like us to be involved in outreach work in our locality. It was Charles Spurgeon who stated: *"The Prayer Meeting is the powerhouse of the church"*. Let us not underestimate the power of prayer.

Finally, there is the '**Proclamation**' of the Word of God, telling others that ***"Christ Jesus came into the world to save sinners"*** *(1 Timothy 1 v 15).* In Nehemiah's day the message went forth concerning the rebuilding of the walls and we read in this passage how the message was heard by others: They ***"heard that we builded the wall"*** *(v1) and* ***"heard that the walls of Jerusalem were made up"*** *(v7).* Let us take this example to proclaim the message of the Gospel so others can hear.

If the Lord is in the work, the evil one will not be too far behind. In Nehemiah's day, he suffered opposition *(v1),* ridicule *(v1, v3)* and threats and anger *(v1, v7)* but with the Lord's help we can overcome these obstacles and opposition. Let us with the help from God, ***"stand against the wiles of the devil"*** *(Ephesians 6 v 11)* and take the encouragement from Paul who suffered in his work for the Lord too - ***"Therefore, my beloved brethren, be ye stedfast, unmoveable, always abounding in the work of the Lord, forasmuch as ye know that your labour is not in vain in the Lord"*** *(1 Corinthians 15 v 58).*

"Go ye into all the world, and preach the gospel to every creature" *(Mark 16 v 15).*

NOTES